Tombstone Tales

Shirley Brokenshaw

Copyright © 2017 Shirley Brokenshaw

ISBN 978-0-9559036-9-4

This edition published in 2017 by Baggywrinkle Productions

First Printing - 2017

'All rights reserved. No part of this publication may be reproduced, stored in a retrieval system, or transmitted, in any form, now known or yet to be invented, or by any means, electronic, mechanical, photocopying, recording or otherwise, without the prior permission of the author.'

Cover design by Artylicious

Printed and bound in the UK by PrintMyBook

Contents

Beginnings	1
Graves, Coffins and Customs	5
Post Mortem Photography	13
Trends and Symbols	16
Inscriptions	24
Disease, Illness and Accidents	28
Babies and Children	34
War, Bombings and Air-raids	35
Ghosts	41
The fear of being buried alive	43
Teignmouth People	45
Poem	71
Reference Sources	72
Map	73

Introduction

Cemeteries have always held a fascination for me. Nothing morbid though! I like to read the inscriptions and always wonder what the people buried there were like. What was that person's occupation? Was the rumour of murder true? How did they die? Why did those children all die within a few weeks of each other? Did that person have an interesting life? Was the ghost story true? Unanswered questions. If only they could speak.

So, after thinking about it for several years, I decided to write a little book and where better to start than at the lovely old Teignmouth Cemetery in South Devon.

Research took many hours, weeks, months. I had to be sure the information was as accurate as could be and, because of the sensitive nature, I needed to contact as many living relatives as possible. This was, firstly, to gain their permission to print details of any relations and, secondly, to perhaps find out more about a particular person. Every family has their stories and it would be lovely to share some of these.

Although some details of most burials are logged, such as names and dates, the stories behind the stones can be lost in time. The idea of this book is to reveal some of those stories, whether they are funny, interesting, or tragic and to fill in some background.

I hope you will enjoy reading this book and find 'Tombstone Tales' as interesting to read as I found to write.

Shirley Brokenshaw

Thanks

The information contained has been compiled using a number of sources and as accurately as possible. Reference sources are listed at the back of this book.

Thanks must go to the following people for their input: author Margaret Graham for inspiring me in the first place; Sandra Windeatt; Marguerite Pipe; Joan Piper; Pauline Street; Stella Small and the staff at the Teignbridge Council Cemeteries Office, Newton Abbot.

Not forgetting, of course, Mike Brokenshaw, who is far more technical than me, and knew where to go to find particular facts. He also did a grand job on researching the Fraser family and for supporting me all the way.

Thank you also, to the Sinclair family and everyone else who supported and encouraged me.

Shirley Brokenshaw

PS Some of you may know that I run a charity called 'Teign Heartbeat' in Devon. We provide Awareness training in CPR and Defibrillator use and act in an advisory capacity to help communities obtain their own Defibrillator Units. £1 from every book sold will be donated to this charity.

Beginnings

The Old Teignmouth Cemetery first opened for burial in 1855. It is situated between Exeter Road and Higher Buckeridge Road in Teignmouth, South Devon.

There are several buildings on the site. These were constructed more than 150 years ago and were designed by noted local architect

Joseph William Rowell. He was born in 1797 and designed many buildings in the South West during his life-time, including The Avenue in Newton Abbot.

Rowell tended to specialise in ecclesiastical work and designed several rectories and churches in the area. Among them was St John the Baptist church at Bishopsteignton and St Pauls, Devon Square, Newton Abbot.

The new cemetery was created to serve the whole of Teignmouth although, until 1909, it was divided into areas for East Teignmouth, West Teignmouth and Shaldon. It was to be overseen by a Burial board.

The following is taken from a newspaper cutting of July 1854.

'The Burial Board for the Parishes of East and West Teignmouth was established on July 7, 1854 and consists of 18 members. Mr W R Jordan is clerk and registrar. The Cemetery, situate about a mile from the town, is about 3 acres, 3 roods and 27 poles in extent. About 2 ½ acres are consecrated. The cost of its formation and the erection of the Mortuary chapels, lodge etc was £4,150'

The Board was responsible for the management of the cemetery and the collection of fees (but not the fees due to any clergy conducting burials).

St James and St Michael's graveyards, Teignmouth, were closed in 1854 after the Buckeridge Road cemetery was made available. Lower down in the town there was often a problem of flooding so it was felt that higher ground was more suitable. Some bodies were moved from the affected areas but I've been unable to trace these to the Old Teignmouth Cemetery in Buckeridge Road.

Unfortunately, moving the cemetery to higher ground was not without its problems, as evidenced by a report in the Exeter and Plymouth Gazette of December 1856.

'A meeting of the Burial Board was held on Thursday last, in the vestry of St Michaels, when it was determined to purchase a hearse, for the use of the friends of deceased parishioners, without any fee, and directions were given to enquire the cost immediately. Many of the poorer inhabitants have often found much difficulty in conveying a corpse to the cemetery, and to such this will prove a great boon.'

The board employed a lodge keeper at the cemetery at a salary of £10 per year. The lodge keeper was required to *'report any destruction or mischief to the board or the clerk.'*

In 1883 notice was given for the removal of bodies from the Myrtle Hill graveyard. These bodies have not been traced but some may possibly be in the oldest part of the Buckeridge Road site.

Not all of the plots would have had a headstone and a number have incurred damage over the years, from the weather and shifting ground. Those that survive do so with varying degrees of legibility that will always cause headaches for the researcher. It is good to see that a 'Friends of Teignmouth Cemetery' group has been set up. Supported by the local council, they are doing sterling work to restore some of its former glory and allow us to remember the stories of those people who are buried here and their place in the history of Teignmouth.

I read recently that, in Lancashire, thieves have been ripping out gravestones from cemeteries and selling them, to unwitting members of the public, as flagstones for gardens and drives. Police likened the crime to grave-robbing and vowed to catch the culprits. I hope they did.

DID YOU KNOW?

Have you ever wondered why some people were buried in unconsecrated ground and others in consecrated ground?

Often this was because the person had not been christened or was not a member of the Church of England. The soul was classed as unclean and not holy.

During research I found a rather sad story of a mother who gave birth to twins – one, a boy, was stillborn and not christened. He was only allowed to be buried in unconsecrated ground. His twin sister lived for one day, was christened, and was therefore eligible to be buried in consecrated ground. The twins ended up being buried together in a corner of a cemetery in an unmarked grave.

Another reason for burial in unconsecrated ground was suicide, or for criminals. In 1823 it was enacted that the body of a suicide should be buried privately, between the hours of nine and twelve at night, with no religious ceremony. This was changed in 1882 when bodies were allowed to be buried at any time.

Graves, Coffins and Customs

The French were first to coin the term 'cofin' taken from an ancient Greek term meaning 'basket'. Since its long use in the funeral industry the meaning evolved and softened over time. In today's modern French language the word more appropriately means 'cradle'.

Around 3150 B.C. ancient Egyptians were already using advanced preservation (embalming) techniques for 'the afterlife'. Archaeologists have found mummies in stone sarcophagi and decorated wooden containers. Sometimes the Kings of that time required their servants to be killed and placed in a tomb with them, to accompany them on their journey. (Domestic life was harsh in those days!)

Around 700 B.C. in Europe, the Celts constructed burial boxes out of flat stones before depositing their dead.

With most early burials mourners interred the body, without any preparation or covering, so that the body could naturally return to Mother Earth. However, some wrapped the body in a crude blanket or shroud.

Later, people began to construct wooden boxes, to hold the deceased, and what would become known as a coffin became the norm. As the boxes became more decorative they were used for display as well as burial[1].

---

[1] The generally accepted difference between a coffin and a casket is that a coffin has 6 sides, whereas a casket is rectangular with four sides.

In 1784, in order to save wood, Austria's Holy Roman Emperor, Joseph II, declared that reusable coffins were to be used. These coffins were made with a trap door on the bottom so that the body would drop into the hole and allow the coffin to be pulled back up and used for another funeral. Following public outcry, the law was repealed within the first six months.

Coffins appear to have been made in lead, for several years, before moving on to zinc and these were often contained in an oak surround. The deceased would have lain in the coffin for a few days before being 'welded' in.

Headstones provide glimpses of our past and reveal historical facts about how local people lived and died. A headstone is normally used to preserve the memory of a loved one and they were originally made of wood. They are also known as gravestones and tombstones, believed to be first used in Roman times and in Celtic cultures.

We recognise a headstone as slabs of stone standing upright, at the head of a grave, but originally it was laid *over* a grave. At one time footstones were also used to mark the end of the grave – this was mainly in the 18th century – probably to deter animals from uncovering shallow graves. Neanderthal graves were covered with large, heavy stones and boulders placed directly on a body.

Some of the stones in the old Teignmouth cemetery have the most beautiful carvings on them. It is such a shame they are gradually being eroded away. The stonemasons were amazing at their craft and it must have taken many hours to produce the results.

DID YOU KNOW?

If you wish to repatriate a body from abroad by air the coffin has to be sealed. However it cannot be lead lined.

This is so it may be x-rayed for contraband

WELL I NEVER!

The word 'Undertaker' conveyed the fact that a body was 'taken under' the earth.

Funeral Parlours would allow photographs to be taken of a loved one in their coffin so that they could be remembered

Part of my research took me to the Cemeteries office in Newton Abbot where they hold the old record books.

Burial references used to state how deep a person was buried. If they had '10 feet' by their name that usually meant the person was buried that deep to leave room for 'two more' in the grave. Therefore '8 feet' might mean that one was already in there and there was still enough room for one more on top. Some bricked graves would hold up to four bodies, instead of the usual three – 6ft, 8ft and 10ft.

By an Act of Parliament in 1847 the minimum depth of burial was specified thus:

'No Coffin containing a Corpse shall, be buried in any Grave within the Limits of the special Act, not being a Vault or Catacomb without at least Thirty Inches of Soil between the ordinary Surface of such Burial, Ground and the upper Side of the Coffin and if the Person having the Preparation or the immediate Charge of the Preparation of the Grave to receive such Coffin permit the. Coffin to be buried in such Grave, or if the Person having the Control of the Burial Ground knowingly, permit any Coffin to be buried in any Grave in which there is not left after the Burial thereof Thirty Inches at the least of Soil measuring from the ordinary Surface of Nuisances such Burial Ground to the upper Side of the Coffin the Person having the immediate Charge of the Preparation of the Grave and the Person having the Control of the Burial Ground in which such Burial is made shall for every such Offence be liable to a Penalty not exceeding Five Pounds.'

Burial entries often stated whether the grave was 'unbricked' or not. Initially this was puzzling but further research soon provided the answer.[2]

A common grave would be a standard earthen grave, in which anyone would and could be buried. The internees would not necessarily have known each other in life. Typical internees would be paupers and those unable to afford anything more personal and grander.

A bricked grave would have a stone or brick foundation at the bottom of the grave and brick or stone linings shoring up the inner walls. The first body would be laid on the foundation and then encased by a brick or stone cover. The next body would be laid on top of that and duly encased with a stone/brick cover, followed by another body, if applicable, on top of that one. For practical reasons, bricked graves would usually hold a maximum of 4 adults, one on top of the other, with each body having its own mini chamber within the grave.

Bricked graves were more expensive than common graves and represented something of a status symbol. However, the point was not to exhibit ones standing for all to see, in the same way that an expensive headstone or monument could be seen by one and all. Rather, it served as an act of assurance to family members and friends that the purchaser of the grave had taken the necessary steps to provide a decent burial for the deceased. Short of carrying out an excavation of a grave, it is impossible to determine whether a grave is bricked or not unless it is stated in the cemetery records.

A vault was, and is, sometimes confused with a bricked grave. In general terms a vault would have been bigger than a bricked grave and could often be entered by walking into it - similar to a mausoleum. In the case of a three-plot vault, the centre plot would

---

[2] This information was found in the on line forum of the Family Tree Magazine. It had been supplied in response to a query in 2012.

form one chamber. To the left and right would be additional chambers for more bodies. However, quite often a vault would not necessarily be a walk-in chamber but a large bricked grave which had one or more additional bricked graves to either side.

Before the 19th century most people were buried on their own land or just outside towns. Later, churchyards were used. When these became full land was set aside for cemeteries.

> **WELL I NEVER!**
>
> In the 1800s most funerals at the graveside would have only men attending.
>
> Whilst they would attend the service it would have been rare for a woman to be present at the actual burial.

Victorian (1837 – 1901) funerals tended to be elaborate affairs. Of course there were no cars in the early days of our cemetery – you would have seen carriages and horses coming up the hill with the mourners wearing black out of respect.

Families would invite both relations and work/business associates. They could also hire professional mourners who would join in the walking procession behind the hearse and horses. It would have been a very quiet and serious time. Unfortunately, in winter, the professionals would expect a good supply of gin to keep out the cold. Their demeanour after this was not always as quiet as the family would have liked.

A basic funeral would cost around £5 in those times and included one coffin; one hearse; one horse and the pillows, linen and bearers. A more expensive funeral, at ten times the price, included a smarter, more robust coffin; four horses and many more attendants all smartly dressed, as well as the hearse and linen.

The Victorians seem to have had a morbid fascination with death and dying. If a family was in doubt about what to wear, or how long to mourn for, then there were numerous publications that could be consulted.

Victorian mourning attire was quite an ordeal and governed by rules. This included parasols; hair clips; fans; purses and suitable clothing for the mourning period. Men would wear black mourning cloaks or, after 1850, dark suits with black gloves and hatbands.

Widows were expected to wear full mourning clothes for 2 years. The horses that pulled the hearses were not only dressed in black but could be dyed black, to fit in with the black trend.

When a family member died it was customary to close the curtains, cover mirrors, and wear black. I remember, in the 1960s, wearing a grey coat with a black armband when my grandfather died. People paid their respect to others and would stand still when a hearse went by.

My husband remembers, in 1963 when his father died, that men stood at the side of the road and removed their hats as the cortege passed.

Superstition was rife in Victorian days. If several members of the same family died, everyone and everything, that entered the house, would wear a black ribbon to prevent the deaths spreading even further. This even applied to dogs and chickens.

The deceased were normally carried out of the house, feet first, so that they wouldn't look back into the house and beckon to someone else, who would have to go along with them.

> **DID YOU KNOW?**
>
> Clocks were stopped, and if necessary reset, at the time of death in domestic houses as respect for the deceased.

The other day I saw a man on television who had taken a family clock to be valued.

He said how strange it was that the clock had, of its own accord, stopped *exactly* when the person who owned it died – it was a family story handed down to him.

Now we know the reason why! Nothing spooky about it at all.

Post Mortem Photography

It is not unusual today to see a photograph of a deceased person incorporated into the memorial headstone, particularly if it is a child or young person. These photographs invariably reflect the person in happier times and provide a lasting memory for the relatives.

However, in Victorian times photographs could be a costly business that only the wealthy could afford. For poorer families it may be that the only opportunity to 'capture' a memory of their loved one was after death. This meant that they would often 'do without' in order to get enough money to pay for a precious photograph and keepsake.

There is a lot of evidence that this was a common practice.

When a photograph was taken, they would even go so far as to 'arrange' the deceased in a family pose, not forgetting of course to dress them in their best clothes.

The deceased would be propped up to make them look as if they were standing, or sitting. This was often done by using apparatus to hold the person in place – the clothing hiding the props so that the finished photograph would look perfectly normal and the person seem alive. Children might be shown with some of their favourite toys, or a workman with the tools of his trade.

Manuals were written explaining how to construct the stands. Although this might sound horrendous today, post Mortem photography was widely accepted as normal in early Victorian times. The photographers even went so far as to paint eyes on the closed eyelids of the deceased and rosy cheeks too – all added to the print after the photograph had been developed.

If you look carefully at this photograph of twins it is more than likely that the one on the right is in fact deceased.

There is a measure of debate nowadays as to the existence of Victorian post mortem photography because pictures of the living also often show props being used. Of course, because of the lengthy exposure times required, props were used for the living to reduce movement during the long photographic process.

Whilst there are certainly some fake photos available on the web, I believe that the many surviving photographs speak for themselves. During my research I came across a newspaper advertisement that shows that the service *was* being offered.

> **J. B. LEATHERS, DAGUERREIAN ARTIST,** respectfully announces to his friends and the public generally, that he is prepared to take Daguerreotypes in his superior style, at the lowest prices of any other establishment in this city or New York. He has made an addition to his room, which makes it the largest and best ventilated room in this city.
>
> Persons wishing a likeness, will find it to their advantage to call and examine his specimens, as all his pictures are warranted to give perfect satisfaction.
>
> Likenesses of invalids, or deceased persons, taken at residences.
>
> Call at 101 Fulton st, junction of Main st.   s8 1w*

Trends and Symbols

Between 1780 and 1860 **Urns** were a popular image on slate and marble and meant to reinforce the mourning of those left behind.

An amazing selection of gravestone designs could be found in the 1800s and there was a transition to marble, from slate, as the 19th Century proceeded and styles changed. Here are some of them.

Around 1800 to 1820 **Sunburst** gravestones were popular. Any showing '**eyes**' peeking up over the horizon were suggesting that the soul rises up to heaven.

If you spot a **weeping willow tree** image on marble or slate then this again emphasised mourning and probably dated between 1800 – 1860.

Some grave-stones used both the tree and an urn together, to reinforce the message perhaps.

Cherubs and angels were used to help lead the deceased 'upward' and symbolised spirituality.

Flowers, ferns, branches, vines and wreathes were very popular designs and

16

this trend went on well into the 1880s.

A **Garland** meant Victory in death.

A **broken bud**, **tree** or **branch** often meant a Premature death – usually found on a young person's grave – a life cut short.

Ivy represented immortality and friendship and the actual plant was often planted along side the grave. Ferns meant humility and sincerity.

Iron Cages – apparently sometimes called 'motsafes' were to stop people crossing graves, having the body stolen, or protection from vampires.

Shells, **bibles**, **hands** and **books** were also used between 1800 and 1880, although not as popular as angels.

You might see a few **obelisks** around, standing high above the other stones. These were used from 1800 onwards and reflected an interest in Egyptian culture.

There is a wonderful example in the Old Teignmouth Cemetery of a very tall obelisk with a hand on top, the finger pointing to heaven showing the way.

A **hand pointing down** depicts sudden death (or can sometimes be a Masonic symbol for a secret handshake)

You might see an **Ankh** on some stones: this is an Egyption symbol of eternal life.

Pyramids also reflected the Egyptian trend and stood for Eternity. Because of the pointed top of pyramids it was thought that the devil had nowhere to sit and linger.

In the 18th century symbols were often used to reflect a person's occupation eg a **saw** or **rake**.

A **winged hourglass** meant 'Tempus fugit' (Time flies).

Hands in prayer – devotion.

Hands clasped - A female hand (with lace at the wrist), is usually on the left side and a male (with cuffs and links, or just plain) is on the right, signifying union, friendship, unity and affection. Used as a sign of farewell, love and friendship, not severed by death. A ribbon may join them. This symbol can also indicate marriage, with one spouse leading the other to heaven or a farewell to an earthly existence. The person who died first holds the other's hand, guiding the spouse to heaven.

Lambs – often found on children's graves

Doves were used in both Christian and Jewish ceremonies and usually represented purity and peace.

Broken Column – this example looks quite strange, until you understand the meaning behind it. It represents the break in earthly to heavenly life. I found a wonderful example of this in the local churchyard. At first it looked like an old pipe stuck in the ground, until I got closer to check it out.

Bugle – representing resurrection and the Military.

Scroll – This is a symbol of Life and Time. Both ends rolled up is indicative of a life that is unfolding but can also mean commemoration or scriptures.

Arrows – mortality

Entwined letters – if you see a capital 'A' and 'O' entwined then the letters stand for Alpha and Omega: the first and last letters of the Greek alphabet – the beginning and end of life.

Three circles interconnected – The Holy Trinity

Draperies (Palls) – this is an expression of sorrow and mourning, symbolic of the drapes sometimes used to cover coffins.

Urns – These symbolise immortality, penitence, or for the soul.

The many different styles of the 1800s also included **ships**[3], **anchors**, **chains** and **flags**[4]. However, if ever you spot any **carved human or animal forms**, dated between 1800 and 1890, then you have found a rare image indeed.

This lady was unfortunately lying next to the plinth that she originally was standing on.

Anchor – Sometimes used as a disguised cross by the very early Christians.

The one shown in the photograph is set amongst rocks and can be an occupational symbol in sea-faring areas.

An anchor, with a broken chain, stands for cessation of life, or the severance and release of the spirit from the body.

(For more of the story behind this memorial see the Arthur Anderson Hill story)

---

[33] There is a very subtle example of this in the Inscriptions section

[4] Many military graves will show these

Materials used around 1855 included marble, Portland stone, Devon and Cornish Granite – popular because it is so resilient to the weather. Home grown granite is often too expensive to be used nowadays. There is only one Cornish quarry left and so today granite is usually imported from India or China in a ready-made lawn style.

There is an interesting report from the Teignmouth Post of 28th January 1921 concerning the unveiling of the new War Memorial on the sea front, between the pier and the lighthouse. The memorial, an obelisk of Dartmoor granite some 4 ½ ft square at the base and 19 ft high, had largely been paid for by public subscription. Because of the extreme marine environment the contractors, Messrs T. H and B. Knight and Sons had, at their own expense of £30, *"done the lettering in beaten lead – the most durable of substances"*.

One fact I unearthed (excuse the pun) is that any zinc metal grave markers do not have any lichen growing on them. Apparently this metal material causes a reaction that prevents the growth. Fascinating. The zinc seems to be either described as whitebronze or blue-grey so I'm not sure if there are different types. Maybe one of you can tell me.

New trends that you might come across

One modern trend is to incorporate a photograph of the deceased. This can be interesting and personable, but especially poignant when it is a child.

A Digital Legacy. Use your smart-phone to scan the code on the grave stone and find out more about the deceased. I haven't found any evidence that this has been used in Devon but, in a few years time, who knows.

Video calls and memorial videos are gradually becoming common place. It is thought that this has a positive effect in bringing together friends and family too far away to attend the funeral.

A Digital gravestone, that allows mourners to view pictures and videos of their loved ones, has been developed in Slovenia. The headstone, which has a 48in touchscreen, displays the dead person's name and date of birth and death when inactive. However, when someone stands in front of it, sensors are activated and it turns into an interactive screen capable of playing digital content. Bioenergija, the company behind the device, is selling the tombstones for 3,000 Euro (£2,600).[5]

Ashes can be turned into trees if one so wishes. Buy a biodegradable urn complete with ashes, seeds and soil. Or – mixed with concrete to make a new habitat for marine life. (I'm not sure how that one works)

Even gem stones can be created from the carbon found from a lock of hair or cremated ashes. Amazing.

Woollen coffins; wicker; willow; biogradeable bamboo; cardboard; fleece – all are present trends.

The tradition for giving flowers has been around for many years. Nowadays it is more common for charitable donations to be requested – around 90%

---

[5] Report in The Times Newspaper 25th May 2017

Inscriptions

Inscriptions were carried out by hand in Victorian times whereas now machines are mostly utilised. However, some of the skills used in the 19th century are sometimes still used.

Sayings on gravestones are called 'epitaphs' and these can be very telling as you will see!

DID YOU KNOW?

Inscriptions on 1800 stones were often 'marked' in marble.

Unfortunately this dissolves over time – a good reason why we need to record all those we can.

During my research I came across some strange and funny inscriptions. Most of these are not local (I didn't want to upset anyone) and they are all actual inscriptions used on tombstones.

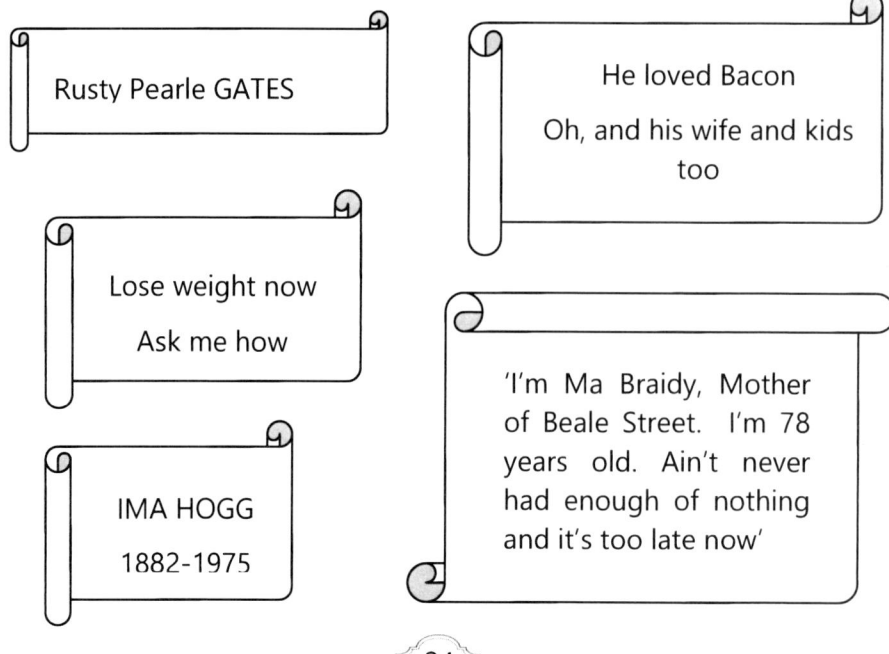

Rusty Pearle GATES

He loved Bacon
Oh, and his wife and kids too

Lose weight now
Ask me how

IMA HOGG
1882-1975

'I'm Ma Braidy, Mother of Beale Street. I'm 78 years old. Ain't never had enough of nothing and it's too late now'

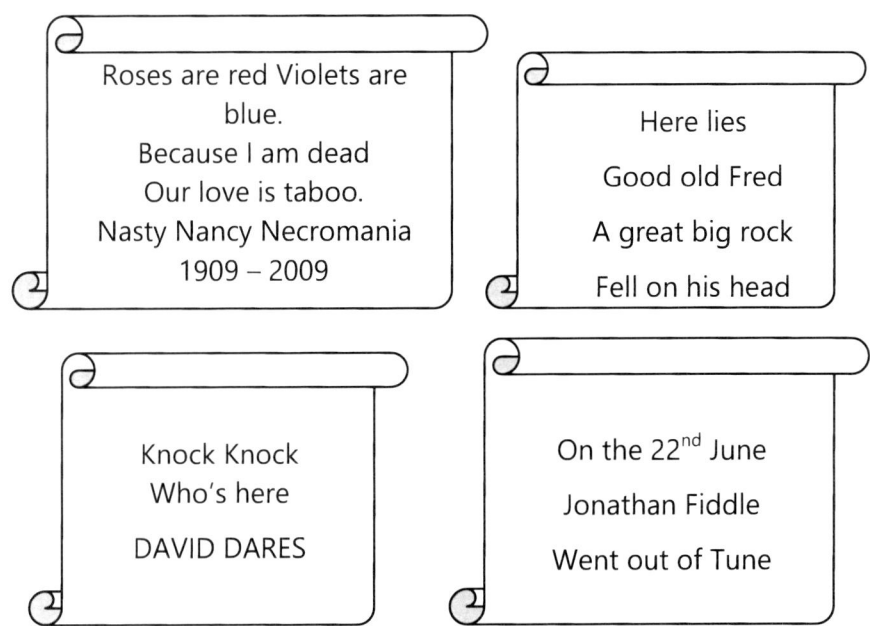

And a really strange one that just says 'FAIL' on the headstone. I wonder what the story is behind *that* stone! Another just says 'SINNER'. Oh dear.

As time went on engravings became more elaborate. It is not unusual to find quotes and poems on headstones but, nowadays, most stones contain only basic details and perhaps a few meaningful words. Within our family history we have an example of how an inscription on a headstone can actually tell you more than the simple words.

Luke Brokenshaw was in the Navy at the 1805 Battle of Trafalgar as Master of the Revenge. He died in 1840 and the eulogy on his headstone[6] has been arranged as the frontal view of a ship under full sail.

---

[6] Luke is buried at St. Michael, Caerhays, Cornwall.

TO THE
Memory
of
LUKE BROKENSHAW
Master in the Royal Navy
Who died on the 3rd. of May

1840

AGED 60 YEARS

For a series of years he distinguished
himself in the service of his country,
and participated in the honors
of a perishable fame.
In the retirement of private life, the milder
virtues were equally conspicuous:
the love of kindred, and that
more extended benevolence
which embraces entire
mankind were his.
He taught both by precept and example, the
obligations of christian duty; and
in the hearts of a long race of
friends and dependants,
his name and memory
are embalmed.
To an open profession of religion, he added
the substantial evidences of a renewed
heart; and at the close of a life of
more than ordinary usefulness,
he esteemed it his greatest
happiness to know he was
'A SINNER SAVED BY GRACE'

Photo - Nigel Hughes

The headstone was badly damaged but has been restored thanks to Nigel and the 1805 Club.

Disease, Illness and Accidents

During the 19th Century disease was rife. Records for this area are difficult to find but, as an example, below is a partial mortality table for one week in London:-

Smallpox	46	Scarlatina	56
Measles	30	Hooping cough(sic)	19
Croup	9	Diarrhoea	7
Thrush	4	Dysentery	1
Influenza	2	Typhus	33
Apoplexy	26	Pneumonia	120
Phthises (sic) or Consumption	120	Cholera	0

This list is not exhaustive, for example it does not include syphilitic eruptions – a regular cause of death. (Nasty!!)

Interestingly there were no Cholera outbreaks logged for quite some time but, when it did strike, mainly in the East End of London, this localised epidemic claimed over five thousand lives.

Industrial Britain was hit by an outbreak of cholera in 1831 – 1832, and also 1848 – 1849. Another cholera epidemic in 1860 swept over the whole of Devon.

There is not a lot of data about the disease in Teignmouth but

Torquay had an outbreak of cholera in 1832 and also an outbreak in 1849, resulting in the deaths of 66 people.

Another killer was TB, that accounted for one third of all those who died in Britain between 1800 and 1850, so there were some horrific diseases around at that time.

Scarlatina and Diptheria was prevelant in Devon during the 1700s.

In 1824 there was a measles epidemic in the South, particularly in Exeter.

1863/64 saw the return of Scarlatina in the South West, followed by a chronic measles epidemic and in the late 1800s / early 1900s a pandemic of influenza spread world wide and millions died.

Those diseases probably account for most of the infant deaths in our cemeteries.

Well I Never!

In the 18th Century Cancer was thought of as purely a female disorder

Sudden Cardiac Arrest

Some reports of deaths in old court records seem to indicate that the cause was from Sudden Cardiac Arrest, although it was not called that then. The reports often said *'deceased fell down and instantly expired'* and *'Death was awfully sudden'* Court Verdicts – *'Died by the Visitation of God'*

Drowning Accident.[7]

Rita and Enid AUSTIN drowned in Teignmouth, near the lighthouse. Rita was only 14 and her sister Enid 19. They died on 13th August 1914. Before moving away to St Margarets-on-Thames their father had previously conducted one of the principal drapers businesses in the town.

A large group of bathers had got into trouble in a rough sea at low tide, requiring a number of both ladies and gentlemen to be helped ashore by rescuers. The sea was too rough for the council boatman, who normally patrolled the bathing area, to launch his boat.

The Coroner enquired as to whose responsibility it was to advise bathers when conditions made the activity hazardous. It was normally done by the operators of the bathing machines.

The coroner asked the Council surveyor if there was a more formal way of indicating unsafe bathing conditions. The surveyor replied that the chairman of the Teignmouth Swimming Club had offered to raise a distinctive flag at the pierhead, whenever conditions were considered unsafe. The council would advertise this through notices posted at the beach and at the bathing machine site.

The Coroner thanked the many rescuers, without whom the tragedy could have been much worse.

Map reference H116 Buried 10 ft & 8 ft.

---

[7] Description taken from the coroners inquest as reported in the Western Times Tuesday 18th August 1914.

Harold Frank RICKETTS

Map reference MM207 8ft.

Harold drowned in Teignmouth in 1916 aged 24. He was a Metropolitan Police Constable and was out in a boat with his wife, mother-in-law, sister-in-law and two children aged four and six, having been married just three weeks earlier. He noticed a boy swimmer in difficulty and tried to help. The boy panicked and pulled Harold under, overturning the Ricketts boat in the process. The rest of the Rickets family were all rescued and the boy's friends rescued the boy, but Harold lost his life. Sadly Harold Ricketts could not swim.

This event is also commemorated in Postmans Park[8], London, a small haven among the office blocks near St Paul's Cathedral and home to the Watts Memorial. Established by Victorian artist G F Watts, it is a monument to 'ordinary heroes' who died saving others. Each of the 117 plaques tells the story of one such act of heroism.

---

[8] Created in 1880 the park gets its name from its proximity to the old General Post Office and because postal workers used it for a stroll in their lunch break.

Polio

Eliza Ann DAVEY died 24 Feb 1920 aged 67 of paralysis. As most of her family seemed to have died from the same complaint I'm wondering if, perhaps, it was polio as there was an epidemic 1920 – 1955 across the country.

In 1928 the Iron Lung was invented. The changing pressure inside the machines enabled patients to breath. Around this time whole wards were often devoted to iron lungs, with just the heads of patients visible. The invention came about too late alas for many residents in Teignmouth and elsewhere.

How sad it is to think of the mortality rate of years ago when modern medicines were not available. Sometimes whole families were wiped out within a few days of each other.

Frederick Cornish FROST

Estate Agent Aged 59

Died May 14th 1914

'Died suddenly from apoplexy. Over feeding and not enough exercise' (Ref Albert Best Diary)

Unbricked grave 10ft

Samuel METHERILL

Shipwright Aged 78

Died Sept 1st 1915

'Slipped over some stairs and shook himself so much that he died of shock'

(Ref Albert Best Diary)

Map reference – LL120

Unbricked grave 10ft

William BOWDEN

Died 16 Dec 1910 Aged 68

William was a long time resident of Teignmouth and described as one of the leading art dealers, and picture connoisseurs, in the West Country. He was found one morning lying at the bottom of the basement stairs at his house in Bitton Street, Teignmouth. The doctor who attended informed the coroner that he considered death was due to a fractured skull and, given Mr Bowdens age, he could not rule out a seizure prior to the fall.

There is an interesting point of social history in that the body was found on a Friday morning and the inquest, complete with County Coroner and Jury, took place on the Saturday. The rapidity of response was most likely because it was the law at that time that the jury had to see the body. This requirement was about to be removed by Parliament but the Coroner insisted that, until the law was changed, he could not dispense with it.   Map reference B16

DID YOU KNOW?

Flowers were originally used, when someone died, to mask the smell of the body decaying.

DID YOU KNOW?

The technique of vaccination, as we know it today, was first tried by Edward Jenner in 1796 as a prevention of smallpox. It was slowly developed, during the 19th Century, to include more diseases but the technology was not as good as that which we enjoy today. Death from disease was much more common until well into the 20th century.

Babies and Children

Apparently, before 1953, stillborn babies had no funeral and were buried with others – they were not required to be registered. If the babies were given a name then possibly there would be a record.

The 1953 registration act came about so that historians and the medical proffession could collect information about still births. Since then a reason has to be given as to why the child did not live.

The tiny body would often be 'put in' or 'alongside' anyone who was being buried that day and the headstones would not reflect this fact, as usually there was no link with the adult who had died.

Lots of infants died at an early age – we are lucky today having modern medical support.

Edwin COYSH

Died Oct 28 1886 - 2 years old

Son of John Coysh, baker.

'Taken poorly at breakfast and got worse so was put to bed. A little later he got convulsions and died in the afternoon'. – (Ref Albert Best's diary).

Map reference F 105

DID YOU KNOW?

Apparently 5 children are killed every decade by a grave-stone falling on them

DID YOU KNOW?

It was customary to decorate the hearse in white, if a young person had died, and in black for anyone of maturity.

War, Bombings and Air-raids

Teignmouth old Cemetery has a significant number of graves of both military and civilian personnel who lost their lives as a direct result of war or conflict. The Commonwealth War Graves Commission (CWGC) maintains a searchable database of those, both military and civilian, buried in the Teignmouth Cemetery. It may be found at:-

http://www.cwgc.org/find-a-cemetery.aspx

Search for Teignmouth and you will get both the military and civilian listings. There are 25 military burials of the 1914-1918 War and a further 24 military and 79 civilian burials of the 1939-1945 War.

In the case of military burials, if a memorial was not provided by the family the CWGC has provided one. Individual graves are marked by uniform headstones. These are differentiated only by their inscriptions: the national emblem or regimental badge; rank; name; unit; date of death and the age of each casualty. Below each inscription is an appropriate religious symbol and a more personal dedication chosen by relatives.

During the Second World War Teignmouth was subjected to a number of Air Raids, comprising of both bombing and strafing attacks. Between July 1940 and February 1944 some 228 houses were destroyed and over 2000 damaged. The location of the targets for these raids – the railway, docks and the Morgan Giles boatyard, all within the town, was always going to result in significant casualties. As a result a total of 81 people were killed and around 150 injured. Of those killed, 5 were serving military personnel on leave, 10 were children aged 16 or under and 35 were 60 or older.

All of these losses are tragic as most of them involve more than one member of the same family and occasionally several generations. I have decided to just highlight a few examples that I believe are particularly poignant.

The first air raid.

Florence Joyce MEDLAND, aged 16, was hit by shrapnel and severely injured in a Teignmouth air raid on July 7th 1940 at Teignmouth pier. She died in Teignmouth Hospital from her wounds a day later on July 8th. Four other children were severely injured.

Florence Joyce had brothers who fought in the war, faced lots of danger, and came home safe and well. Ironic that young Florence Joyce, at such a young age, should die at home, where she should have been safe.   Map reference CC82

Air Raid., March 2nd 1941. A whole family was wiped out at 47 Second Avenue – Leslie HOOK, a RNR Seaman home on leave, his wife Dorcas (both 29) their little daughter Delphine aged 3, together with Dorcas' parents, Frank and Elsie FIELD. They are all buried together in Teignmouth cemetery at Map reference SS12

The Hook family grave

Teignmouth Hospital Bombed on 8th May 1941. Seven patients were killed, 5 of them elderly, together with three nurses.

Bombing on 2 Gloucester Road. 2nd July 1942. Dick SMITH was home on leave, before going back to fight in the Royal Naval Patrol Service, when he was killed at the family home along with two of his family.

CAN YOU HELP?

Victoria Cross. This chap, as far as I know, never lived in Teignmouth but was called Teignmouth MELVILL. I have yet to find out if there was any connection. Teignmouth was born Sept 1842 in Marylebone, London and died 1879 in South Africa aged 36. Fighting in the Anglo-Zulu war he was awarded the VC posthumously for gallantry in the face of the enemy. You may have seen him portrayed in the film Zulu Dawn where he was played by James Faulkner.

Does anybody know how he got his name?

Leonards Story

Amongst the graves in the Teignmouth Cemetery, listed by the CWGC, is that of Leonard Arthur George Hamlyn aged just 16, the son of Arthur and Nora Hamlyn of 2 Mulberry Street Teignmouth. Leonard was a Junior Canteen Assistant in the NAAFI and, according to the War Graves Commission listing, he was serving on HMS Centurion. The newspaper report of his funeral states that he died on the 22nd April 1941 as a result of an air raid in Plymouth[9]. This was intriguing so I searched a little deeper.

---

[9] Leonard died 22 April 1941 at the Prince of Wales Hospital, Greenbank,

HMS Centurion was a King George V class Dreadnought battleship of some 26,000 tons, built in Devonport Plymouth and originally commissioned in May 1913. She took part in the Battle of Jutland and was decommissioned under the Washington Agreement in 1926. She then had her armament removed and became a radio controlled target ship. She was very well suited to this role due to the thickness of the Armour on her deck and sides.

Early in 1941 it was originally decided to use her as a block ship to block the Mediterranean harbour of Tripoli, which was being used as a base by the Italians and Germans. However, she was converted into a likeness of H.M.S. Anson, a battleship at that time under construction in Portsmouth, in order to confuse the German intelligence.

In Devonport Dockyard her magazines were converted to carry fuel, a dummy funnel was erected and an aircraft hanger of wood and canvas was built. She now carried three gun turrets, complete with 14 inch guns all made of wood and canvas which, from a distance, looked realistic. Six inch guns were painted on the side of the dummy hanger. When all this work had been completed, she was a fair likeness of H.M.S. Anson, at least from a distance[10].

This work was carried out and completed in April 1941. She was commissioned on the 26th April and sailed, with a crew of 16 officers and 265 men, on the 4th May on the trip around the Cape to Bombay.

During the time that this work was carried out, Plymouth in general and Devonport in particular, were being subjected to intense air raids.

---

[10] Janet King - 'WW2 People's War' - an online archive of wartime memories, contributed by members of the public and gathered by the BBC. The archive can be found at www.bbc.co.uk/ww2peopleswar'

The raids that took place on 21st/22nd April 1941 were particularly notable as there was a direct hit on an air raid shelter, in Portland Square, killing 72 people who had taken refuge there.

We do not know if Leonard was killed on the ship, in the dockyard, or perhaps in the town enjoying a last run ashore prior to his ship becoming operational. Centurion survived the rest of the war as a decoy ship, and her final action was to be scuttled as a protection to the Mulberry Harbour during the Normandy landings.

Leonard's headstone carries the NAFFI crest, as you can see in the picture. His funeral service, at the Gospel Hall Teignmouth, was attended by the Chairman and two other representatives of Teignmouth Urban Council.

Leonard's grave[11] may be found at Map reference CC84.

---

[11] It has recently been announced that his grave has been adopted and will be tended by the Canonteign Sea Cadets unit based in Teignmouth

DID YOU KNOW?

The Devonshire Cemetery in France is unique in that it contains the graves of soldiers from a single regiment who all fell on the same day (1st July 1916), on the Somme, as the result of an enemy attack.

Three days later the Germans were forced back and the Devons collected their dead from no man's land.

A mass grave was fashioned out of the support line trench where they went over the top, and a wooden plaque was set up reading...

'The Devonshires held this trench, The Devonshires hold it still'.

The present cemetery, directly over the grave, was consecrated in the 1920s. 160 men (10 unidentified) from the 8th and 9th Battallion, The Devonshire Regiment, are commemorated by two long rows of headstones overlooked by a simple stone cross.

Ghosts

Do not read the following if you are of a nervous disposition!

Apparently the Buckeridge area of Teignmouth is haunted, so early manuscripts would lead us to believe. A Mr R W Wakefield, at number 7, is logged as saying "unholy things ride along Buckeridge Road at night". I have found no date for this quote but 'the ghostly happenings' probably stem from the late 1800s when there would have been carriages along that road.

Ropes of sand: a Teignmouth penance

There are a number of stories about the beach at Teignmouth being haunted by the ghost of Sir Warwick Hele Tonkin as he carries out his penance of making ropes of sand.

What is not clear is, if true, why this unfortunate gentleman acquired what is designed to be a never ending task.[12]

Sir Tonkin died about 1860. He was connected with the shipping business, a magistrate, friend of Louis Napoleon and built a theatre for the town.

His obituary doesn't suggest anything controversial:

'Death of Sir Warwick Hele Tonkin: This gentleman died on Friday evening at the advanced age of 86. The deceased was the son of the late Mr. Warwick Hele Tonkin, of Exeter, and married the only daughter

---

[12] The ropes will be destroyed by each incoming tide requiring the task to be started all over again.

of the late Mr. Thomas Mitchell, M.D., formerly of Chudleigh, who died about five years ago without issue. Sir Warwick was a Major in the army, but never, we believe, saw much active service. Subsequently, he was a barrack-master at Exeter for a number of years. In 1826 he received a gold medal of the 1st class, from Charles X of France, for aid in a case of shipwreck, he was nominated Chevalier of the Legion d'Honour in 1838 for similar services. He was a magistrate and deputy-lieutenant of the county of Devon. In politics the deceased was a Whig, and a warm supporter of the late lord-lieutenant of the county. He was also Lieutenant-Colonel of the 1st Devon Brigade of Volunteer Artillery, and took a very warm interest in the volunteer movement. The flags of the vessels in the harbour and at different parts of the town were hung at half-mast, out of respect for the deceased knight, who was of a kind and genial disposition, which had endeared him to a large circle of friends. He had lived at Teignmouth for about 40 years. [13]

Sir Tonkin appears to have been an accomplished linguist and musician; and his 'Warwick Clavichord' invention (or Musical Chart), published in 1830, looks interesting. It was what we'd now call a multimedia music learning aid and it mapped notes of the scale, to colours of the spectrum, in aid of 'impressing them more sensibly on the scholar's memory'

Lord and Lady Tonkin were good friends of the well-known Brays of Tavistock, and Anna Eliza Bray dedicated the 1846 edition of her novel *Courtenay of Walreddon* to Lady Tonkin. Sir Tonkin was also an acquaintance of the Sidmouth antiquarian Peter Orlando Hutchinson and the Keats brothers.

---

[13] Morning Post (London, England), Tuesday, September 15, 1863; pg. 5; Issue 28001. 19th Century British Library Newspapers: Part II.

The fear of being buried alive

The fear of being buried alive was rampant in the late 1700 and 1800's. This was due in part to the cholera epidemic and rumours that live burials had occurred. People would often sit with their dead, for hours, just in case they could see any signs of life. This fear would be so strong that sometimes instructions would be left to 'leave the coffin open for two days' just to make certain they really were dead. Edgar Allen Poe's story *'The Premature Burial'* didn't help matters.

In response to these fears a safety coffin was developed. The coffin would include a mechanism that allowed the occupant to signal that s/he had been buried alive. Usually it was a cord attached to a bell.

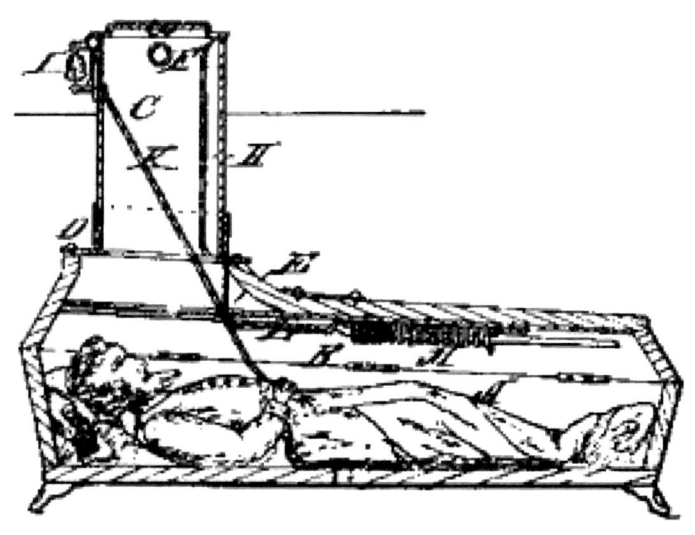

For a naval burial at sea the body was sewn into a weighted hammock. It was traditional that the last stitch was taken through the nose just to check that they were actually dead!

This was not without good reason. Writing of his experiences at the battle of Trafalgar William Robinson, from Farnham, Surrey (HMS Revenge), described how, in clearing away the dead, the crew nearly jettisoned overboard the ship's cobbler *'a very merry little fellow, the very life of the ship' company, for he was the mirth of the mess, and whatever duty he was ordered his spirit made light of the labour'*. Unconscious, he was about to be thrown out of the gunport as dead when he began to kick and twitch, which saved him.

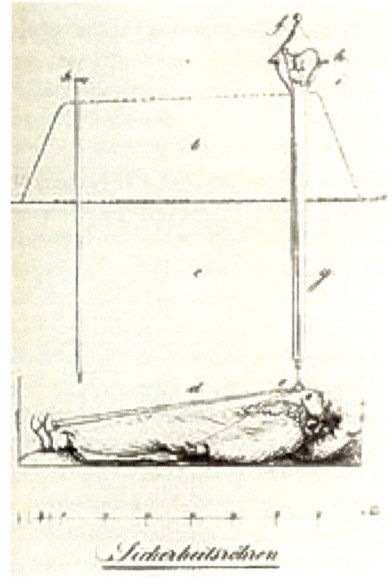

Teignmouth People

There are a large number of interesting people connected with Teignmouth. Here are just a few examples.

Albert Best

In Teignmouth library I came across the diaries of Albert Best and was so riveted I could hardly put them down. Do read them if you get the chance – they are fascinating.

Albert was born in Teignmouth in 1840 and died in 1920 aged 80. He lived at 23 Bitton Street, then Russel Lane, Sun Lane, and then 32 Bitton Street. Albert was a Whitesmith, gas fitter, builder and plumber, and carried out a lot of work in and around Teignmouth building up his business. By the time he died he was an important man responsible for much of the work here, including our local drainage, a resevoir on Dartmoor and not forgetting the many hours of voluntary work he carried out.

When you next wander around Teignmouth take a look at the drain covers. You may just see A. Best on some of them. Now I must admit that I've never had an interest in drain covers before but, since reading Albert's Diaries, I can't help but look out for them, I've included some photographs.

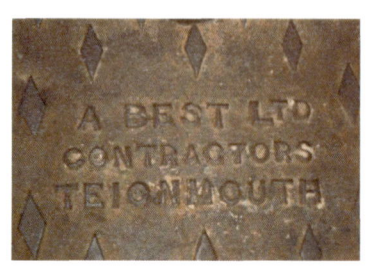

Albert was, unwittingly, a wonderful help in my research because he actually made a lot of the coffins used in the burials and, the odd comment or two, helped build up a picture of life in the 1800s.

Albert has a prominent place in the Old Cemetery, Teignmouth and is buried close to, and just north of, the former chapel. He shares the grave with his parents and the headstone is a huge block of granite from Dartmoor.

When I went hunting for Albert's last resting place I knew I was looking for a slab of granite. In my mind was a picture of my kitchen with its black sparkling, shiny granite worktops – wrong! Albert's stone is an enormous slab of brown granite roughly hewn around the top.

Throughout this book I have popped in little snippets of interest, some of which include comments from Albert. His diaries were mostly factual but some of his comments were priceless.

This is a picture of a lavatory pull handle found in an outhouse at Woodway House, Teignmouth, clearly showing Alberts name. This also provides a convenient (sorry) link to our next gentleman who actually built Woodway House, long before Albert was in business.

James (Jack) Spratt

Jack Spratt lived in Trafalgar Cottage, and then Woodway Cottage/House, in Teignmouth. He was a Commander in the Royal Navy and a hero at Trafalgar. Jack was born in 1771 and died in 1852 aged 81.

When Jack was 25 he joined the Royal Navy and is best known for his exploits, aged 34, at the Battle of Trafalgar in October 1805. There were 27 ships led by Admiral Lord Nelson. Spratt was on HMS Defiance as a Master's mate (later being made a lieutenant after the battle for his bravery).

During the battle Spratt got badly injured in one of his legs. The surgeons wanted to amputate his leg but Spratt refused. He was taken to hospital in Gibraltar and thrashed about so much, due to the pain, that his leg was encased in a box – locked so that he could not cause any more damage.

Because he complained so much about the pain the box was

eventually opened. To everyone's surprise there were hundreds of maggots feeding on his injured leg – most were one inch long and buried up to their necks in Spratt's leg. They all had to be cleaned out.

With the benefit of modern science we now know that those maggots probably saved his leg, because they would have cleaned out the wounds, but in those days it must have been quite a shock to find them. After 17 weeks he was discharged – his leg was saved but remained 3 inches shorter than the other.

What a character Jack Spratt was. He retired to Teignmouth, married a local girl, and was well known for his exploits at long distance swimming, once swimming from Teignmouth to the Ore Stone. It is reputed that, unable to ride a horse because of the injury sustained at Trafalgar, he was often seen around town riding a donkey. He was still swimming at the age of 80.

Thomas Vernon Woolaston

Born 9th March 1822 in Lincolnshire, died 4th January 1878 in Teignmouth, at 1 Barnpark Terrace. The house no longer stands as it was damaged during WW II and subsequently demolished.

He was a prominent English entomoligist and malacologist[14] and a close friend of Darwin. After graduating from Jesus College Cambridge in 1845 he was made a fellow of the Linnean Society[15]. Wollaston spent the winter of 1847–1848 in Madeira, returning for his Cambridge M.A. graduation in 1849. In the years to 1855 he made four long trips to Madeira followed by trips to the Canary and Cape Verde Islands. His last trip was to St Helena with his wife. On his return poor health forced him to move from London to Devon.

Following his death his principal collection, of Madeiran Coleoptera, was purchased by the then Oxford University Museum (now Oxford University Museum of Natural History). The British Museum purchased his principal collection of Canarian Coleoptera.

Although Thomas Woolastion lived and died in Teignmouth I have found no cemetery record of him being buried here despite entries in biographical notes to the contrary.

---

[14] One who studies Molluscs

[15] A non-political and non-sectarian institution, existing solely for the furtherance of natural history. It is the oldest natural history society in the world.

William Frederick Yeames

Born 18th Dec 1835 in Taganrog Russia. The son of the British Consul.

Died 3rd May 1918 in Teignmouth aged 82.

William Yeames was a British painter. He usually painted in oils and the painting he is most well known for is 'And when did you last see your father?' (1878).

You can see this in the Walker Art Gallery, Liverpool. There is also a life-size waxwork tableau of the scene in Madame Tussauds, London.

Thomas Luny

Thomas Luny was born in 1759 and died on 30th September 1837 in Teignmouth. You can see his house in Teign Street where there is a sign on the wall acknowledging this. He would have had some jolly good views from there, to inspire him in his work. Luny was a well-known, and accomplished, Marine painter having served his apprenticeship under marine artist Francis Holman. He moved to Teignmouth in 1807 and, between then and his death, produced over 2,200 paintings. His work is even more remarkable when you realise that he had a crippling disability (arthritis) in later life that affected his hands. It is said that, confined to a wheelchair, he could only hold a brush using two hands or by having the brush strapped to his wrist. Incredible.

His sketches and paintings reflected his vast knowledge of ships - amassed whilst travelling, and it was probably because Teignmouth was such an interesting coastal port that attracted Thomas Luny to eventually live here.

Thomas Luny is not buried in the Old Teignmouth Cemetery but in the churchyard of St James the Less, that is not far from where he lived.

His memorial is shared with his half brother Captain James Wallace RN who died in 1832 aged 76.

Thomas Luny's memorial in the churchyard of St James.

The Ness Teignmouth – Thomas Luny

Arthur Anderson Hill

At first glance one would think that Arthur Hill's memorial shows him as a seafarer. However, the entry in the cemetery register describes him as a 'Gentleman'. He was only 31 when he died so who was he and what was his connection with Teignmouth?

Map reference Q 125

Arthur was born December 1854, in Firgrove, Hampshire, the youngest son of Thomas Hill Esq.
In 1876, in Winchester, he married Agnes Sadler (b1854 Chobham, Surrey). Living in Shepton Mallet in Somerset they had 3 children, Albert A (1877), Kathleen A (1879) and Montague A (1880).

Arthur's father, Thomas, was a partner, with William Gorton and Francis Christopher Hill, Arthur's elder brother, in a company of sugar refiners, based in Southhampton, called Hill, Garton and Co.

In 1871 the company bought, at auction, a Shepton Mallet brewery trading as 'The Anglo-Bavarian Brewery' that claimed to be the first brewers of lager in the UK.

In October 1879 Lt A. Hill resigned his commission in the 1st Hampshire Rifles Volunteer Corps (Territorials) as I suspect he was about to become more involved in the running of the brewery.

Since the closure of the brewery in 1920 the site, now Grade II listed, has been used for storage and is now divided into units as a trading estate.

In 1881 the Southhampton partnership of Hill, Garton and Co was dissolved by mutual consent and its assets and liabilities divided between two new companies.[16]

The Anglo-Bavarian Brewery Company was to be under the control of Thomas Hill and William Garton.

---

[16] London Gazette 1881

The Saccharum manufacturers and sugar refiners Garton, Hill, and Co. was to be run by William Garton and Francis Hill in conjunction with William's sons Richard and Charles.

The Garton family, as well being in the sugar business, were also brewers. Charles Garton (Snr) had a brewery in Bristol.[17]

In the 1881 census Arthur, his wife, family and four servants are living in Bowlish House, Shepton Mallet. In the census his occupation is given as 'Brewer' but he was probably much more than that.

Bowlish House, now a hotel and restaurant, is a large Georgian building completed in 1732, extended in the early 1800s and for eighty years used as the residence of the brewery manager, a more senior position than current usage of the word would indicate[18]

---

[17]. The Charles Garton Bristol brewery was ultimately acquired by Anglo-Bavarian in 1898.

[18] The drawing room of Bowlish House was used as a location during the filming of the TV series Broadchurch

Thomas Hill, now aged 71, is living in a large house (called 'The Rock') at Reigate in Surrey. He is described in the 1881 census as 'Justice of the Peace' so it is unlikely that he has taken on the day to day management of the brewery.

It must be fairly safe to assume that, in 1881, Arthur was running the Shepton Mallet brewery for his father but why, between then and his death in 1887, did he suddenly move to Teignmouth? We know that he was not just visiting as it states in the Probate records – *'Arthur Anderson Hill late of Teignmouth'*

His personal estate is given as £5,467 4s 8d. If we convert that to a 2017 figure, it is 'worth today' about £4.26 million pounds. Not bad for a 31 year old.

Arthur's memorial includes reference to his late father, his wife Agnes (1854 -1911) and his three children; Montague (1880 – 1911); Albert (1877 – 1905); and Kathleen (1879 – 1975).

As yet I have found no clues as to why he was in Teignmouth - maybe here came here for health reasons. In 1881 he was still living and working in Shepton Mallet We know that his father probably died in 1883 at which point Arthur may have chosen to retire. Teignmouth had certainly built a reputation as a healthy place to live, but at that time he was only 28 years old and, unless he had a significant illness, he was very young to be giving up work.

It is pure conjecture on my part but I notice that his two sons subsequently died at 31 and 28 respectively. Maybe there was a family medical reason for them all dying so young. Without their death certificates we shall probably never know.

The Fraser Family - Teignmouth.

There is one particular gravestone, in the old Teignmouth Cemetery, that has always interested me. It shows three siblings dying in the same year, two of them within a few days of each other. The family name is Fraser.

I wanted to find out more about the family and why the children died, within months of each other, and so young – it seemed very sad - so I enlisted help to research the facts. The following is the product of that research.

Map reference E 9

In Loving Remembrance
Of
DONALD FRASER
WHO DIED MARCH 2ND 1875
AGED 9 MONTHS
ALSO
HARRY FRASER
MARCH 13TH 1875
AGED 2YRS 5 MONTHS
ALSO
MARY GARDNER FRASER
DECEMBER 13TH 1875
AGED 8 MONTHS
BELOVED CHILDREN OF MATTHEW & MARY FRASER
He shall gather the lambs with His Arm, and carry them in His bosom
ALSO
ALICE AND WALTER
WHO DIED IN INFANCY
AND
JANE NORTHEY
WHO DIED DECR 8TH 1898
AGED 72
A BELOVED FRIEND OF THE FAMILY
FOR 27 YEARS
ALSO
ELLEN GEAKE
OUR BELOVED SISTER
WHO DIED AT WALTHAMSTOW AUGUST 1903

Any headstone can invoke an element of sadness, as it

commemorates the loss of a loved one. However, there are those that immediately make one think that someone has had more than their fair share of grief. A perfect example of this is the stone erected by the Fraser family that commemorates five children, a family friend and a sister.

What follows is a brief account of the life of some of those associated with this annus horribilis.

Matthew and Mary Fraser were not famous in the generally accepted way, but their story has many of the interesting elements that make it worth investigating and recording.

Matthew Fraser was born in 1842 to Matthew and Biddy. The 1851 census shows him living with his mother (a Laundress), plus two brothers and a sister in Honiton. In the 1861 census, now 18 years old, he is living in Launceston with his uncle, Alexander, who describes himself as a Draper and Tea Dealer.

In 1871 Matthew is still living in the same house as his uncle, who by this time has retired, but at 28 Matthew has his own household.[19]

This consists of Matthew as head, occupation Draper; his 25 yr old sister Lissie, occupation Assistant; Henry Gardner (30) Partner; a servant girl Catherine Tucker (19) and a visitor Mary Prout (15). Mary was born in the same place as Catherine so in all probability was visiting her.

One assumes that Matthew is now running the family Drapers business. Interestingly, according to the census return, his business partner, Henry Gardner, was born in the same place as Matthew's

---

[19] This was what we would now call a 'house in multiple occupation'. Even where it was all the same family, the census recorded each household separately.

mother Biddy. A little more investigation shows that Gardner was in fact Biddy's maiden name, so Henry was almost certainly a relation, probably cousin to Matthew.

1871 was also of significance for Matthew as it was the year he married Mary Geake. She was not quite the girl next door but six doors away is close enough. Mary was also 28 yrs old and a draper's assistant. Presumably this was in her own family's business as her father was a retired draper, local councillor and member of the school board. One can only speculate that he may have given Matthew a hard time enquiring of his prospects.

Following their marriage Matthew and Mary moved to Teignmouth where they, not surprisingly, opened a Drapers business, initially we believe at 5 Bank Street[20].

All their 9 children were born and registered in the Newton Abbot district. Here are their birth years.

Harry	1872	Alice	1880
Donald	1874	Herbert	1882
Mary Gardner[21]	1875	Alexander	1884
Kate	1876	Walter	1886
Helen	1879		

---

[20] Whites Trade Directory 1878

[21] It was very common at this time to use family surnames as middle given names for children.

Unfortunately, as we know from the headstone, 5 did not survive past infancy.

In March 1875 Donald (9 months) and Harry (2 yrs 5 months), passed away, followed by Mary Gardner (8 months) in December the same year. That year must have been so traumatic for Matthew and Mary. To lose your first three children in the space of one year is almost unimaginable let alone losing one at Christmas whilst carrying a fourth.

Given their ages and that Donald and Harry died within a week or so of each other makes one suspect that the cause was some form of illness. With, one assumes, a successful business Matthew and Mary were not exactly paupers so the most likely explanation is some form of infection.

Around 1840 the government had introduced a body known as the Improvement Commissioners. This was a committee of local people of standing, charged with overseeing improvements in living conditions by the introduction of underground sewers and the availability of clean drinking water. This inevitably came at a cost and was covered by the levy of a rate on local property. Property owners had a responsibility to keep drains clear, to prevent overflow of sewage, and the Commissioners had the power to prosecute offenders. Those found guilty could be fined or even sent to jail.

The Commissioners in Teignmouth were very active, even at one point utilising the redundant cast iron pipes from Brunel's Atmospheric Railway as underground sewage pipes[22].

---

[22] Woodway Road.

As if the traumas of 1875 were not enough Matthew and Mary lost a further two children, with the deaths of Alice in 1880 and Walter in 1886. In both of these cases the death was registered in the same Quarter as the birth so it is quite likely that they may have been associated with birth issues.

Despite these setbacks it appears that the Fraser's business was thriving, as evidenced by the census return for 1891. Matthew and Mary are now 48 years old and have moved just along the street to 10/11 Wellington Street,[23] that we must assume are larger premises. Luckily the Frasers, and their employees, were living over the shop so the census gives us an idea of the size of his business.

As well as Mathew, Mary, their two sons Herbert(9) and Alexander(6), a general domestic servant and a nursemaid, there were seven other employees living on the premises, comprising 5 drapers assistants, a milliner and a dress maker. There is also a visitor, Blanche Hewett (27) High School Headmistress who is Mary Fraser's niece. There is no sign on the census of the two girls Kate and Helen.

This is the first time that we come across Jane Northey, drapers assistant, who is remembered on the headstone as a family friend of 27 years who died in 1898.

Moving on to 1901 the business is still at 10/11 Wellington Street, Teignmouth, and all four children are working in the business, together with another 3 drapers, a milliner and a dressmaker. They also have a cook, housemaid and general servant. The cook is Mary Richards who was with them in 1891 but then as a general servant.

Mary's brother Joseph Geake is visiting.

---

[23] These premise are occupied today by the clothes shop Peacocks.

In the last census available (1911), at the time of writing, Matthew, Mary, Kate and Alexander are, with two servants, living at a house called Brimley the rear of which today backs onto Higher Brimley Road[24].

Matthew at 68 is obviously still involved in the business, describing himself as – Draper, dressmaker and milliner. Mary is also still involved as she is Draper – Assisting in business. The two children are both listed as Draper (Partner).

On the 20th April 1913 Mary passes away and, one could say, is spared the anxiety of her two remaining sons enlisting and going off to war.

Herbert enlisted and was part of 179 Siege Battery, Royal Garrison Artillery (RGA) who operated the large howitzers used in bombardments. The 179 was sent to France and, between October 1916 and March 1917, was firing daily in the battle of Ypres. He was mentioned in despatches - not for any heroics on the battlefield - but for saving a man from drowning in the sea. The following is the 1917 citation on his service record.

'The GOC has much pleasure in recording the gallant conduct of No.128365 Gunner Fraser. An NCO of 201 Seige Bty RGA, when assisting to bring in some men who were in difficulties when bathing was carried out to sea beyond the sea wall. ??? Walker reached him but was too exhausted to bring him in. Gnrs Fraser and Marchant by the exercise of the greatest coolness and courage managed to get through with a rope and rescue the two men.'

---

[24] This property is listed and a description may be found in the website of listed properties www.britishlistedbuildings.co.uk . Alternatively just Google 'Brimley Teignmouth'.

Coincidentally Alexander also enlisted in the RGA and was posted to 201 Seige Battery, although we have no way of knowing if he was present at the incident involving his brother.

By the time of their enlistment both brothers were married and, on their return, settled in Teignmouth. Herbert was living at 2 Brimley Villas and Alexander at 6 Grovenor Terrace.

In 1906 Matthew had become a Land Tax Commissioner and in later life he was a Justice of the Peace[25].

DEATH OF MR. MATTHEW FRASER AT TEIGNMOUTH.

The death occurred somewhat suddenly at his residence, Brimley, Teignmouth, on Tuesday night, of Mr. Matthew Fraser, draper and silk mercer, whose business premises are situate in Wellington-street. Deceased had been in his garden with his two sons, and on sitting down in his room expired during a conversation. He was 85 years of age. Mr. Fraser was born at Honiton, and after a short period in business at Launceston, came to Teignmouth in 1871. He was head of the firm of Messrs. M. Fraser and Sons. Of a most genial disposition, deceased was well known and highly respected. He was the senior magistrate sitting on the Teignmouth Bench, having been appointed in 1912. For half a century he was treasurer of the Congregational Church, and a fete in aid of its funds was to have been held in his grounds on Thursday. He was a lifelong Liberal and President of the Teignmouth Liberal Association.

Matthew Fraser died June 28th 1927 leaving an estate of £15,619 (worth about £4.6M at today's prices). His obituary appeared in the Western Times 1st July.

---

[25] Kellys Directory 1923

Matthew and Mary are buried together in the Old Teignmouth Cemetery. Herbert Fraser died in 1947 aged 64 and Alexander in 1962 aged 78.

M. Fraser and Sons, General Drapers 10 Wellington Street, Teignmouth, was still listed in the telephone book in 1957 (Telephone No. Teignmouth 50).

This small example shows that, hidden behind the tombstones, there is a world of ordinary people trying to make a living, doing their bit for mankind and surviving all the pains and disappointments that life can throw at them.

The Windeatt family – Teignmouth

There were a number of Windeatts living in and around Teignmouth in the 18th and 19th centuries, and also in Shaldon, Exeter and Weston Super Mare. Several are buried in the old Teignmouth cemetery. Some of the family lived in Lower Brook Street in West Teignmouth and can be traced back as long ago as the 1700s. Just a few of the cottages in Lower Brook Street are still standing as that area was bombed during the war. There was a John and Tamazine Windeatt (married 1802) who became Fruiterers and Greengrocers in Bank Street, Teignmouth. Details are patchy because the registration of births, deaths and marriages did not become compulsory until 1837.

One of the family was John and Tamazine's eldest son John Windeatt (1805 – 1885) and his wife Mary Ann (nee Froom) (1809 – 1884). They married in 1830, in Exeter cathedral, and eventually had ten children. Initially they lived in Exeter and 1834, aged 29, John was arrested for 'unlawful assembly' and here is part of what one newspaper reported...

Unlawful Assemblies and a Secret Society

'...a number of workmen had been arrested at the Sun public-house, where they had assembled for the purpose of forming an illegal secret society; that 15 of them ... had been committed to gaol, and that on Friday, after another examination, they had been remanded till Tuesday...' '...The delegates are Daniel GILL and James STODDART, of London, bricklayers; ... the Exeter men are Thomas BRICE, Samuel SKOINS, Richard CORNELIUS, John STURRIDGE, James HUGHES, W. CRUSE, W. GAY, George BLACHFORD, John WINDEATT, John JENKINS, William STOCKER, Thomas LEE, and John MAJOR. They were informed that they would be admitted to bail on providing good and sufficient

sureties... On Wednesday morning the mayor and magistrates again assembled at the prison, and the whole of the persons charged...'

- The Examiner (London, England), Sunday, February 2, 1834; I Issue 1357

John may have been a Chartist Sympathiser as this extract from The Northern Star and National Trades might indicate. The column was entitled 'Chartist Intelligence' –[26]

'On Monday the 7th inst . . . In the evening the band and several friends - over forty - sat down to a good substantial supper, at Mr. WINDEAT's Temperance-house'.

Mary Ann had her moments too. A certain Polly Ponsford threatened to throw Mary into a river but didn't succeed: a formidable couple.

As well as his political activities John was able to turn his hand to several different skills in the building trade. He worked as a plasterer, roofer and slater in Exeter, declaring himself as a 'hellier' in 1837, when his second son John Benjamin died. (Probably Hillier - a roof tiler?) Possibly this sad event prompted a move to Teignmouth in time for the birth of their daughter in 1839, also called Mary Ann.

John, Mary Ann and 5 children were living in Teignmouth in 1841, probably finding more opportunities for work there, as John's uncle George had a building firm in Shaldon, not far away. They were living in Fore Street at this time.

At the 1851 census John gives his occupation as an 'Eating and Coffee House Keeper' so he seems to have given up the building trade. In

---

[26] Chartists saw themselves fighting against political corruption and for democracy in an industrial society, but attracted support beyond the radical political groups for economic reasons, such as opposing wage cuts and unemployment

the same census, John and Mary's third son, Charles Allen (1837 – 1897), was still at school – unusual at 15 years old in those days as they would normally be apprenticed or, if from a poor family, in service or labouring.

Charles A became a jeweller, maybe working locally for his uncle in Regents Place, although it seems his first love must have been music because he had a couple of pieces of music published and eventually became a full-time musician and a Professor of music. Later, when Charles married, and had children, their family proved to be very musical with one becoming violinist and several others working as musicians.

In 1852 John has another change of profession, as reported in the Exeter flying post.

' IMPROVEMENT COMMISSIONERS - On Tuesday evening last, a meeting of the Commissioners took place at the Clerk's Office, Mr. E. CROYDON In the chair. Mr. WINDEATT of Fore street was elected waterman by a majority of one; there were several applicants for the office. The committee appointed at a former meeting to inquire into the necessity for a new watering reported that a new cart was indispensable, and one had therefore been ordered.'

-Trewman's Exeter Flying Post or Plymouth and Cornish Advertiser (Exeter, England), Thursday, May 13, 1852; Issue 4507

In 1861 John was 'Waterman to Reservoir' and Mary Ann was 'Refreshment House Keeper'.

Just after the census in the summer of 1861, Charles' Uncle Richard went bankrupt and moved back to Exeter. If Charles A was working for him life would have been difficult as he had married in 1858, had a young son, also called Charles, and another baby due before the end of the year. It looks like he was able to continue his profession as they went on to have more children and on the birth certificate for his son Corelli (1868) Charles's occupation is listed as Jeweller. Charles and his family eventually moved to Weston Super Mare becoming well known for their musical performances.

The 1871 census shows him as an 'Eating & Coffee House Keeper.' By this time all ten children had been born.

When the 1871 census was taken Charles and his family were living in Fore Street, Teignmouth, next door to his parents and two of his sisters, Charlotte and Mary Ann II. His parents also had two lodgers, Frederick and Arthur Slocombe, both from Dawlish, plasterers and probably brothers. Frederick, although only 26, was a widower and formed a relationship with Charlotte – it seems he got his wicked way with her by apparently promising marriage. The result was an illegitimate daughter for Charlotte.

In 1872 she went to court to sue the father for 'breach of promise' – and won the case. This was a very unusual, and brave, thing to do for a young woman in those days. I daresay her father, John Windeatt, helped and encouraged her. She was represented by two barristers, one a QC, as well as a solicitor, so the family must have been doing pretty well financially. The jury awarded Charlotte £150. If we convert that to a 2017 figure it is worth today over £100,000. Mr Slocombe filed for bankruptcy shortly afterwards!

By the time of the 1881 census John, now 75, is still working as a Municipal Sanitary Inspector.

John and Mary Ann died in 1884 and 1885 and are buried in the Teignmouth Old Cemetery at H51 (8ft and 6ft), although I have been unable to find a headstone.

Mary Ann II, John and Mary's daughter, I believe died in 1908 and was buried on 10th Dec (Map reference J165 6ft). There is also buried in the same plot (N88) a Henry Windeatt (4th July 1886 8ft) and, in the same plot, Jane Godbeer Windeatt (13th October 1889 6ft).

There are a few Windeatts buried in Shaldon too - four year old William Windeatt Cole buried 18th Nov 1856; George, aged 30, 7th Feb 1837; Frederick Francis, aged 3 months, 12th June 1844: William Hamlyn, aged 39, 6th June 1850: and George, aged 71, 25th Nov 1852.

My research showed links with Bishopsteignton, Exeter, Totnes, and beyond, for the Windeatts. They had a whole range of occupations:- writing books; game keeping; farming and more. One Thomas Windeatt, in 1807, wanted stones for a farmhouse at Fox Tor Farm. Shame he dismantled an ancient monument to get them!

An interesting, strong minded, and clever, family.

This is a token typical of a Temperance Coffee House. Maybe it was the one belonging to John and Mary Ann. There was a Globe Tavern in Teignmouth in 1874 but I unfortunately don't have an address.

Poem

Stella Small lives in Teignmouth and is a wonderfully imaginative poet and writer. She wrote a poem entitled 'A Cemetery – What does the word say to you?' and here is part of her poem, written especially for this booklet.

A Cemetery

A place of sorrow, of grieving, loss and tears?
But it can also be something else
A place of peace – somewhere to stir the memory and pay tribute.
A ritual destination for the bereaved to celebrate a happy life now ended

Headstones stretch away in lines like rows of uneven teeth
Some small, some tall, but all will honour those who lie beneath.
Graves lie neatly side by side positioned head to toe
Some are carefully tended and love will surely show
But others lie forgotten and neglected in the row

Epitaphs expressing love and everlasting peace
Eternal rest and promises that love will never cease
But those who lie beneath won't see
Those symbols of sincerity

Nor will they see the starlit nights
Or hear the wind and rain
The occupants feel nothing – be it pleasure or pain
Won't see the ever changing clouds that drift across the sky
Nor hear the whisper of the wind as it blows softly by.

The older plots have headstones that are chipped and mouldered green
Where words are a long since worn away, and rarely ever seen
Whenever there is death – and death will always be
Then there will always be a place for tender memory.

Reference Sources

Albert Best's Diaries.

The Cemetery Office, Brunel Road, Newton Abbot.

Teignmouth Library reference books.

Family History newspaper archives

Various Geneology websites

Wikipedia

The Windeatt family history website

Map

Teignmouth Old Cemetery

The identification of individual areas relates to the records held by the Teignbridge Council Burial Office

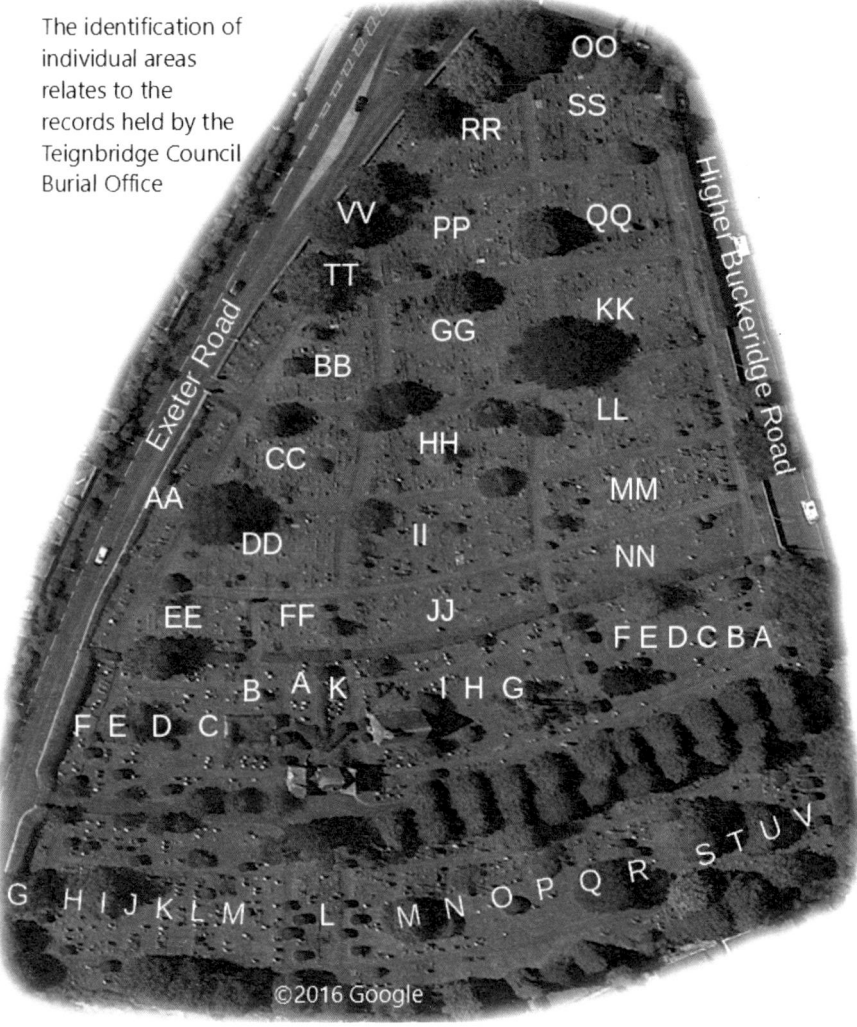